Traditional CHRISTMAS *favorites*

Darcie Anzalone

BARBOUR
PUBLISHING

ISBN 1-59310-882-6

Cover image © Getty Images/Food Pix

Published by Barbour Publishing, Inc., P.O. Box 719, Uhrichsville, Ohio 44683 www.barbourbooks.com

Our mission is to publish and distribute inspirational products offering exceptional value and biblical encouragement to the masses.

Member of the
Evangelical Christian
Publishers Association

Printed in Canada.
5 4 3 2 1

CONTENTS

Time was with most of us, when Christmas Day,
encircling all our limited world like a magic ring,
left nothing out for us to miss or seek;
bound together all our home enjoyments, affections, and hopes;
grouped everything and everyone round the Christmas fire,
and made the little picture shining in
our bright young eyes complete.

CHARLES DICKENS

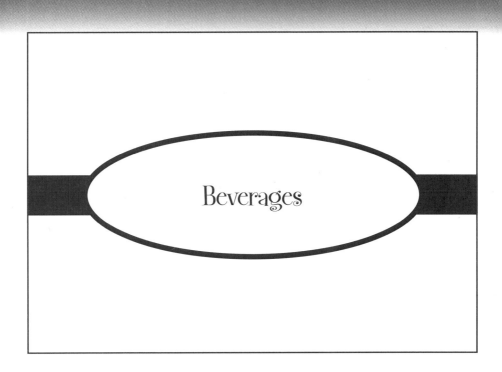

Beverages

Coffee Slush

3 cups strong coffee, hot
2 cups sugar
1 pint half-and-half

1 quart milk
2 teaspoons vanilla

Dissolve sugar in hot coffee. Cool completely. Add remaining ingredients and blend well. Freeze mixture. Thaw for two hours before serving.

Creamy Dreamy Hot Chocolate

1 (14 ounce) can sweetened
   condensed milk
½ cup unsweetened cocoa powder

2 teaspoons vanilla
⅛ teaspoon salt
6½ cups hot water

Combine first four ingredients in large saucepan; mix well. Over medium heat, slowly stir in water. Cook until heated through, stirring frequently.

Eggnog Punch

1 quart sherbet, any flavor, softened
2 cups orange juice
2 cups pineapple juice

1 quart eggnog
Additional sherbet

In large mixing bowl, beat sherbet until smooth. Mix in orange and pineapple juices. Gradually pour in eggnog and blend thoroughly. Pour mixture into a punch bowl and scoop additional sherbet to float on top.

Hot Apple Cider

2 quarts apple cider
8 whole cloves

8 whole allspice
1 stick cinnamon

Combine ingredients in large saucepan. Bring to a boil. Reduce heat and simmer, uncovered, for 10–20 minutes. Remove spices before serving.

Hot Cranberry Cider

1 quart apple cider
1 (32 ounce) bottle cranberry juice
½ cup lemon juice

½ cup firmly packed light brown
    sugar
8 whole cloves
2 cinnamon sticks

Combine ingredients in large saucepan. Bring to a boil. Reduce heat and simmer, uncovered, for 10 minutes. Remove spices before serving.

Wassail

2 quarts apple juice
2 cups orange juice
1 cup lemon juice
1 (18 ounce) can pineapple juice

1 stick cinnamon
1 teaspoon ground cloves
½ cup sugar

Combine ingredients in large saucepan. Bring to a boil. Reduce heat and simmer, uncovered, for 1 hour. Serve warm.

Christmas may be a day of feasting, or of prayer,
but always it will be a day of remembrance—
a day in which we think of
everything we have ever loved.

AUGUSTA E. RUNDEL

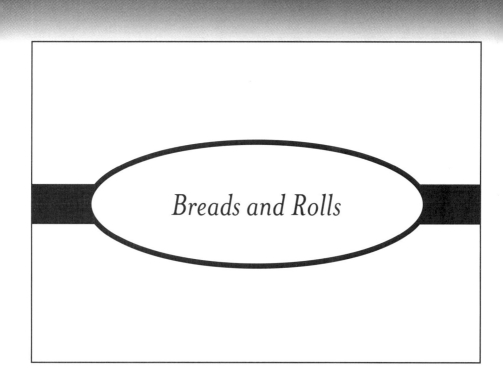

Breads and Rolls

Chocolate Chip Sour Cream Banana Bread

½ cup butter
1 (3 ounce) package cream cheese
1 cup sugar
2 eggs
2 teaspoons vanilla
1½ cups flour

1 teaspoon baking soda
½ teaspoon salt
1 cup mashed bananas
½ cup nuts, chopped
1 cup mini chocolate chips
½ cup sour cream

Preheat oven to 350 degrees. Cream butter, cream cheese, and sugar. Mix in eggs and vanilla. Gradually add dry ingredients. Stir in mashed bananas, nuts, chocolate chips, and sour cream. Divide into two greased loaf pans and bake for 1 hour.

Cranberry Scones

1¾ cups flour
1 tablespoon baking powder
½ teaspoon salt
1 cup quick or old-fashioned oats
½ cup butter
½ cup chopped pecans

½ cup dried cranberries
½ teaspoon dried orange peel
⅓ cup honey
¼ cup milk
1 egg, lightly beaten

Preheat oven to 375 degrees. In medium bowl, mix together flour, baking powder, salt, and oats. Cut butter into dry ingredients. Mix in pecans, cranberries, and orange peel. In small bowl, whisk together honey, milk, and egg. Pour wet ingredients over dry and stir with fork just until dough begins to hold together. Turn dough out onto floured surface and gently knead 8–10 times. Pat dough into circle. Place on greased cookie sheet. Cut dough into wedges and separate them slightly. Bake for 10–12 minutes or until light golden brown.

Cranberry Walnut Streusel Bread

1½ cups flour
1 teaspoon baking soda
1 teaspoon baking powder
1 teaspoon ground cinnamon
½ teaspoon salt
1 cup sugar
2 eggs, lightly beaten

2 tablespoons butter or margarine, melted
2 teaspoons orange zest
½ cup orange juice
1 cup fresh or frozen cranberries
½ cup chopped walnuts
½ cup raisins

STREUSEL:
  ¼ cup flour   ½ teaspoon cinnamon
  2 tablespoons sugar   2 tablespoons butter

Preheat oven to 350 degrees. Grease and flour loaf pan. In small bowl, stir together flour, baking soda, baking powder, cinnamon, and salt. In large mixing bowl, beat together butter, sugar, eggs, and orange zest. Alternating between wet and dry, gradually mix in the dry ingredients and orange juice. Stir in cranberries, nuts, and raisins. Pour into prepared pan. In small bowl, cut butter into flour, sugar, and cinnamon mixture. Sprinkle over bread batter. Bake for 1 hour 15 minutes or until toothpick inserted in the center comes out clean. Cool for 10 minutes, then remove to wire rack to cool completely.

Dinner Rolls

1 cup butter
1 cup sugar
1 cup milk
2 packages dry yeast
1 cup warm water

1 teaspoon sugar
2 teaspoons salt
2 eggs, lightly beaten
6 cups flour
Melted butter

Over low heat, melt 1 cup butter with 1 cup sugar and milk. Remove from heat and cool to lukewarm. In large mixing bowl, dissolve yeast in warm water with 1 teaspoon sugar. Mix in butter mixture, then salt and eggs. Blend thoroughly. Gradually stir in flour. Place in greased bowl; cover and let rise until doubled. Punch down; form into rolls, then place on greased baking sheets and let rise again. Brush tops with melted butter and bake 9–12 minutes or until golden at 350 degrees.

Festive Bubble Loaf

¾ cup butter, divided
½ cup brown sugar
1 small jar maraschino cherries,
   drained and coarsely chopped

1 cup pecan halves
1 cup sugar
2 teaspoons cinnamon
1 (24 count) package frozen
   dinner rolls

In microwave-safe bowl, melt ¼ cup butter. Stir in brown sugar. Pour into bottom of well-greased tube pan. Place cherries and pecans over sugar. Melt ½ cup butter; stir in sugar and cinnamon. Roll each frozen roll in cinnamon-sugar mixture. Arrange in tube pan. Cover and let rise overnight. Bake at 350 degrees for 30 minutes. Cool 10 minutes, then invert onto serving plate.

Oatmeal Dinner Rolls

1 cup quick-cooking or old-fashioned
oats

3 tablespoons butter
2 cups boiling water

Place oats and butter in large mixing bowl. Pour in boiling water and let mixture stand for 20 minutes.

2 packages dry yeast

⅓ cup warm water

In small bowl, dissolve yeast in warm water.

In another bowl, mix together:

3/4 cup brown sugar

1 tablespoon sugar

1½ teaspoons salt

4 cups all-purpose flour

1–1½ cups whole wheat flour

Stir yeast into oatmeal mixture, then gradually mix in dry ingredients. Add enough flour to form a soft dough. Cover and let rise until doubled; form into dinner rolls and place in greased baking pans. Let rise again until double. Bake at 350 degrees for 20–30 minutes.

Orange Rolls

BASIC SWEET DOUGH RECIPE:

2 cups water, lukewarm
½ cup sugar
2 packages yeast
2 cups flour

¼ teaspoon salt
2 eggs, beaten
½ cup vegetable oil
4½ cups flour

Mix water, sugar, yeast, 2 cups flour, and salt and beat until smooth. Add eggs and oil. Mix well. Stir in remaining flour and combine thoroughly. Let rise 30–40 minutes.

FILLING:

Melted butter or margarine
¾ cup sugar

¾ cup coconut
1–2 tablespoons orange zest

Roll half of dough into circle. Brush with melted butter. Sprinkle half of sugar mixture over butter. Cut into wedges and roll each wedge into a crescent. Place in greased 9x13 inch baking pan. Repeat with remaining dough. Let crescents rise; bake at 350 degrees for 25–30 minutes. Pour hot glaze over warm rolls.

GLAZE:
  ¾ cup sugar   ¼ cup butter or margarine
  4 tablespoons orange zest   Additional coconut
  ½ cup sour cream

Boil first four ingredients for three minutes. Pour over warm rolls. Sprinkle rolls with coconut.

Overnight Cinnamon Rolls

1 cup milk
1/3 cup butter
2 packages active dry yeast
1/2 cup sugar

4 1/2 cups all-purpose flour
1 teaspoon salt
3 eggs, lightly beaten

FILLING:
3/4 cup brown sugar
1 tablespoon ground cinnamon

1/2 cup chopped pecans

In small saucepan, heat milk until it bubbles. Remove from heat and stir in butter until melted; let mixture cool. In large mixing bowl, dissolve yeast in milk mixture. Stir in sugar, 3 cups of flour, salt, and eggs. Gradually add remaining flour, 1/2 cup at a time, stirring well after each addition. When dough pulls away from sides of bowl, turn it onto a lightly floured surface and knead until smooth, about 8 minutes. Lightly oil a large mixing bowl. Place dough in bowl; turn to coat with oil. Cover with damp cloth and let rise in warm place until doubled in volume, about 1 hour. Punch down dough and turn onto a lightly floured surface; roll into a 10x14 inch rectangle. Lightly brush one long edge with water. In small bowl, combine cinnamon and brown sugar and sprinkle over dough. Sprinkle chopped nuts over dough. Roll dough into a log, rolling toward the damp edge; seal the seam. Cut dough into 12 equal pieces; place pieces in greased 9x13 inch baking pan. Cover with plastic wrap and place in refrigerator to rise overnight. In the morning, preheat oven to 375 degrees. Let rolls stand at room temperature for 30 minutes before baking them for 25–30 minutes or until golden.

GLAZE:
  1 teaspoon light corn syrup   1¼ cups sifted powdered sugar
  ½ teaspoon vanilla   2 tablespoons half-and-half

Meanwhile, combine corn syrup with vanilla in small bowl. Whisk in powdered sugar and enough half-and-half to make a thick glaze; set aside. Drizzle glaze over warm rolls.

Honey Whole Wheat Bread

3 cups boiling water
1½ cups old-fashioned oats
¾ cup honey
6 tablespoons vegetable oil
3 packages dry yeast

½ cup warm water
5 cups whole wheat flour
2½ cups unbleached white flour
3 teaspoons salt

Pour 3 cups boiling water into large mixing bowl. Stir in oats; allow mixture to cool to lukewarm. Add honey and oil. Dissolve yeast in ½ cup warm water, then add to oatmeal mixture. In another mixing bowl, combine flours and salt. Stir 6 cups of flour mixture into oatmeal mixture. Gradually knead in additional flour to make a soft dough. Knead an additional 5–10 minutes. Let rise in covered bowl until double. Punch down dough, then knead again for 5–10 minutes. Form into loaves and place in greased loaf pans. Let rise 30 minutes. Bake at 325 degrees for 1 hour. Cool on wire racks.

Never-Fail Crescents

1 cup milk, lukewarm
½ cup vegetable oil
½ cup sugar
1 teaspoon salt

2 packages dry yeast
3 eggs, beaten
4½–5½ cups flour

Mix first six ingredients; let mixture sit for 15–20 minutes. Gradually add enough flour so that dough pulls away from sides of bowl. Cover and let rise until dough doubles in size. Divide dough into three sections. On a floured surface, roll out dough into circle and cut into eight triangles. Roll each triangle into a crescent shape and place on greased baking sheet. Let crescents rise, approximately 1 hour. Bake at 375 degrees for 10 minutes or until light golden brown.

Good news from heaven the angels bring,

Glad tidings to the earth they sing:

To us this day a child is given,

To crown us with the joy of heaven.

MARTIN LUTHER

Cakes and Cookies

Delicious Apple Cake

1½ cups vegetable oil
2 cups sugar
3 eggs
3 cups flour
1 teaspoon baking soda
1 teaspoon salt

1 teaspoon cinnamon
2 teaspoons vanilla
3 cups diced apples
1 cup chopped walnuts or pecans,
    optional

Mix together first three ingredients. Add remaining ingredients and blend well. Pour batter into greased 9x13 inch baking pan. Place pan in cold oven, then heat to 350 degrees. Bake 40–45 minutes. Pour topping over warm cake.

TOPPING:

½ cup butter	1 cup brown sugar
¼ cup evaporated milk	

In small saucepan, bring topping ingredients to a boil. Boil until thoroughly combined. Pour over warm cake.

Fruit-and-Nut Cake

1½ cups flour
1½ cups sugar
1 teaspoon baking powder
1 teaspoon salt
2 pounds walnuts, coarsely chopped
1 pound Brazil nuts, coarsely
   chopped

2 pounds pitted dates, coarsely
   chopped
1 (8 ounce) jar maraschino cherries,
   drained and coarsely chopped
5 eggs, beaten
1 teaspoon vanilla

Preheat oven to 325 degrees. In large mixing bowl, sift together flour, sugar, baking powder, and salt. Add nuts, dates, and cherries. Stir well to coat. Combine eggs and vanilla, then mix into flour mixture. Spoon into three well-greased loaf pans. Bake for 1 hour.

Chocolate Caramel Cake

1 package chocolate cake mix,
   any variety
1 jar caramel ice cream topping

1 (14 ounce) can sweetened
   condensed milk
1 (8 ounce) carton whipped
   topping, thawed

Bake cake according to package directions in 9x13 inch pan. While cake is still warm, poke holes in cake using the handle of a wooden spoon. Pour caramel topping over warm cake, then pour sweetened condensed milk over cake. Cool completely, then frost with whipped topping.

Pumpkin Sheet Cake

2 cups all-purpose flour
2 teaspoons baking soda
1 teaspoon cinnamon
½ teaspoon salt

1 (15 ounce) can pumpkin
2 cups sugar
1 cup vegetable oil
4 eggs, lightly beaten

Preheat oven to 350 degrees. In small bowl, mix together dry ingredients. In large mixing bowl, beat together pumpkin, sugar, and oil. Add eggs and mix well. Add dry ingredients to pumpkin mixture, blending thoroughly. Pour batter into well-greased 15x10x1 inch pan. Bake for 25–30 minutes. Cool completely.

FROSTING:
1 (8 ounce) package cream cheese, softened
¼ cup butter or margarine, softened
1 teaspoon vanilla

2½ cups powdered sugar
3–4 teaspoons milk
Chopped pecans, optional

Beat together cream cheese, butter, and vanilla. Gradually add sugar and blend well. Add milk slowly, just enough to reach spreading consistency. Frost cooled cake and sprinkle with chopped pecans if desired.

Gingerbread

2 cups flour
1½ teaspoons baking soda
2½ teaspoons ground ginger
½ teaspoon allspice
¼ teaspoon salt

⅔ cup molasses
⅔ cup sour cream
½ cup butter, softened
½ cup brown sugar
2 eggs, lightly beaten

Preheat oven to 350 degrees. Grease and flour 9 inch square baking pan. In small bowl, mix together flour, baking soda, ginger, allspice, and salt. In another small bowl, mix together molasses and sour cream. In large mixing bowl, cream butter and brown sugar. Add eggs and beat well. Alternating between wet and dry ingredients, gradually add flour and molasses mixtures. Beat well after each addition. Pour batter into prepared pan. Bake for 30–35 minutes or until cake pulls away from sides of pan and a toothpick comes out clean.

Turtle Cake

1 package German chocolate
   cake mix
½ cup butter
1 (14 ounce) package caramels

½ can (7 ounces) sweetened
   condensed milk
¾ cup chopped pecans

Preheat oven to 350 degrees. Prepare cake according to package directions. Pour half of batter into greased and floured 9x13 inch baking pan. Bake for 15 minutes. Meanwhile, in microwave-safe bowl, melt together butter, caramels, and sweetened condensed milk. Cool mixture slightly, then pour over baked half of cake. Sprinkle caramel mixture with pecans. Pour remaining cake batter over pecans. Bake for 25 minutes.

Buttermilk Cookies

3½ cups flour
1 teaspoon salt
1 teaspoon baking soda
1 teaspoon baking powder
1 cup butter or margarine

2 cups sugar
2 eggs
1 cup buttermilk
Milk
Colored sugar sprinkles

In small bowl, blend dry ingredients. In a large mixing bowl, cream together butter and sugar. Add eggs. Slowly mix in dry ingredients, alternating with buttermilk. Chill dough for at least two hours. Drop by teaspoonfuls onto greased cookie sheets. Dip the bottom of a glass into milk and press lightly on each cookie, flattening slightly. Sprinkle with colored sugar. Bake at 350 degrees for 8–10 minutes.

Candy Cane Cookies

2½ cups flour
1 teaspoon salt
1 cup butter, room temperature
1 cup powdered sugar

1 egg
1 teaspoon peppermint extract
1 teaspoon vanilla
½ teaspoon red food coloring

Preheat oven to 350 degrees. In small bowl, combine flour and salt. Set aside. In large mixing bowl, cream butter and powdered sugar until fluffy. Add egg, peppermint extract, and vanilla; beat until smooth. Gradually add dry ingredients and stir until thoroughly blended. Divide dough in half. Mix red food coloring into half of dough, stirring until coloring is even. For each cookie, shape about two teaspoons of plain dough into a 4-inch rope by rolling it back and forth on a lightly floured surface. Repeat with colored dough. Place plain rope and red rope side by side, press them together lightly, then twist together. Place cookies on greased cookie sheets and curve one end to form a candy cane shape. Bake for 8–10 minutes or until set.

Chocolate Chip Cookies

1 cup butter or margarine, softened
1 cup vegetable oil
1 cup sugar
1 cup brown sugar
1 egg
1 tablespoon milk
2 teaspoons vanilla

3½ cups flour
1 teaspoon salt
1 teaspoon baking soda
½ cup oatmeal
1 (12 ounce) package semi-sweet
    chocolate chips

Mix ingredients by hand in the order given. Do not beat. Drop by tablespoons onto ungreased cookie sheets. Bake at 350 degrees for 9–12 minutes or until cookies are lightly browned.

Lu Ellen's Sugar Cookies

2½ cups flour
1 teaspoon cream of tartar
1 teaspoon baking soda
1 cup butter

1½ cups powdered sugar
1 teaspoon vanilla
1 egg

Preheat oven to 350 degrees. In small bowl, combine flour, cream of tartar, and baking soda. Set aside. In large mixing bowl, cream together butter, powdered sugar, and vanilla. Add egg and mix well. Gradually add flour mixture and blend thoroughly. Chill for at least two hours. Roll out chilled dough on floured surface and cut into desired shapes. Bake for 8–10 minutes.

Jam Thumbprint Cookies

½ cup butter, room temperature
⅓ cup sugar
1 egg yolk
1 teaspoon vanilla

1⅓ cups flour
¼ teaspoon salt
Jam or preserves, any flavor
Finely chopped nuts

Preheat oven to 350 degrees. In large mixing bowl, cream butter until light. Add sugar and beat until fluffy, then beat in egg yolk and vanilla. Gradually mix in flour and salt. Dough will be very firm. Shape dough into 1-inch balls and place on greased cookie sheets. With your thumb, press an indentation into the center of each cookie. Bake for 7–9 minutes or until firm. Remove from oven and fill each cookie with about $1/2$ teaspoon of jam, then sprinkle with chopped nuts. Return cookies to oven and bake for 6–8 minutes or until edges of cookies are light golden brown. Let cookies cool on baking sheet 2–3 minutes before removing to cool on racks.

Russian Tea Cakes

1 cup butter
½ cup powdered sugar
1 teaspoon vanilla
2½ cups flour

¼ teaspoon salt
¾ cup pecans or walnuts,
    finely chopped
Additional powdered sugar

Preheat oven to 400 degrees. Cream together butter, sugar, and vanilla. Gradually mix in flour, salt, and nuts. Shape into 1-inch balls and place on greased cookie sheets. Bake for 15–18 minutes. Roll hot balls in powdered sugar. Let cool, then roll in sugar again.

Soft Ginger Molasses Cookies

4 cups flour
1 tablespoon baking soda
2 teaspoons cinnamon
2 teaspoons ground ginger
½ teaspoon ground cloves
¼ teaspoon salt

¾ cup vegetable shortening
¾ cup sugar
¾ cup dark molasses
¾ cup sour cream
2 eggs, lightly beaten
Additional flour

Preheat oven to 350 degrees. In medium bowl, mix together 4 cups flour, baking soda, cinnamon, ginger, cloves, and salt. In large mixing bowl, cream the shortening and sugar until light and fluffy. Beat in the molasses; add sour cream and eggs and beat until smooth. Gradually stir in dry ingredients; mix until thoroughly combined. Chill dough. Sprinkle work surface with additional flour. Form dough into 1-inch balls and roll in flour. Place on greased cookie sheets and bake for 8–10 minutes or until set.

Velvet Cut-Out Cookies

2 cups butter, softened
1 (8 ounce) package cream cheese,
    softened
2 cups sugar

2 egg yolks
2 teaspoons vanilla
4½ cups flour
¼ teaspoon salt

Preheat oven to 350 degrees. In large mixing bowl, cream together butter, cream cheese, and sugar until light and fluffy. Add egg yolks and vanilla; mix well. Gradually stir in flour and salt. Chill for two hours. Roll dough out on floured surface and cut into desired shapes. Place on greased baking sheets and bake for 9–12 minutes at 350 degrees. Cool on cookie sheets before removing to wire racks. Frost if desired.

FROSTING:
- 4 tablespoons butter, softened
- 1 (3 ounce) package cream cheese, softened
- 3 cups powdered sugar, divided
- 3 tablespoons milk
- ½ teaspoon vanilla
- Food coloring, optional

In mixing bowl, beat together butter, cream cheese, and 1 cup powdered sugar until smooth. Add in milk and vanilla. Gradually mix in remaining powdered sugar and beat until smooth and spreadable. Divide frosting and tint with food coloring if desired.

Christmas Eve was a night of song that
wrapped itself about you like a shawl.
But it warmed more than your body.
It warmed your heart. . .filled it, too,
with melody that would last forever.

BESS STREETER ALDRICH

Candies and Confections

Caramel Popcorn Balls

¼ cup butter
½ cup light corn syrup
1 cup brown sugar
⅔ cup sweetened condensed milk

1 teaspoon vanilla
5 cups popped corn, unpopped
   hulls removed

Combine butter, corn syrup, and brown sugar. Bring to a boil. Stir in sweetened condensed milk and return to a boil, stirring constantly. Remove from heat and stir in vanilla. Pour over popped corn and stir to coat. With buttered hands, form into balls. Place on waxed paper to set. Makes about 15 popcorn balls.

Chocolate Peanut Butter Cup Bars

1 cup butter or margarine, softened
4 cups powdered sugar
1 cup crunchy peanut butter
1 cup graham cracker crumbs
1 (12 ounce) package semi-sweet
    chocolate chips

In mixing bowl, blend first four ingredients together. Press into buttered 9x13 inch baking pan. In microwave-safe dish, heat chocolate chips for 1 minute. Stir. Heat 30 seconds longer or until chocolate is completely melted. Spread evenly over peanut butter mixture. Chill until chocolate is firm.

Cheese Blintzes

1 (1 pound) loaf white bread
¾ cup sugar, divided
2 teaspoons ground cinnamon
2 (8 ounce) packages cream cheese,
   softened

2 egg yolks
1 teaspoon vanilla
½ cup butter, melted

Preheat oven to 350 degrees. Trim crusts from bread and roll each slice flat. In small bowl, combine ¼ cup sugar and cinnamon. Set aside. In large mixing bowl, beat softened cream cheese, egg yolks, ½ cup sugar, and vanilla until smooth. Spread this mixture onto each slice of flattened bread. Roll bread slice up. Dip each roll in melted butter, then roll immediately in sugar-cinnamon mixture. Cut rolls into 1-inch pieces. Arrange the blintzes on greased cookie sheet. Bake for 10 minutes.

Christmas Cinnamon Candy

2 cups sugar
1 cup light corn syrup
½ cup water

½ teaspoon red food coloring
½ teaspoon cinnamon oil

In heavy saucepan, combine sugar, corn syrup, and water. Cook until candy reaches the hard-crack stage, 285 degrees. Remove from heat and stir in food coloring and cinnamon oil. Pour onto greased pan and let cool completely. Break into pieces.

Date Nut Rolls

1 pound crushed graham crackers,
   divided
1 pound miniature marshmallows

1 pound diced dates
2 cups chopped walnuts
2 cups whipping cream, whipped

Set aside ½ cup crushed graham crackers. Fold remaining graham cracker crumbs, marshmallows, dates, and walnuts into whipped cream. Form mixture into rolls and roll in reserved crumbs. Wrap rolls in plastic wrap and chill overnight before slicing.

Divinity

4 egg whites, room temperature
½ teaspoon cream of tartar
4 cups sugar

1 cup water
1 cup light corn syrup
2 teaspoons vanilla extract

Beat egg whites. When foamy, add cream of tartar and beat until stiff peaks form. Boil sugar, water, and corn syrup until candy thermometer reads 250 degrees. While constantly beating egg whites, slowly pour half the syrup over them. Boil the remaining syrup to 280 degrees. Again, beat egg whites while slowly pouring in the rest of the syrup. Stir in vanilla. Let mixture set until cool. Drop by spoonfuls onto waxed paper.

Hopscotch Candy

1½ cups peanut butter
3 cups butterscotch chips

1 (10 ounce) bag mini marshmallows
1 cup chow mein noodles

Melt peanut butter and butterscotch chips over low heat. Remove from heat and stir in marshmallows and noodles. Drop by spoonfuls onto waxed paper. Cool.

Orange Balls

½ cup butter, softened
3½ cups powdered sugar
1 (6 ounce) can frozen orange
   juice concentrate

1 box vanilla wafers, crushed
1 cup chopped pecans
1 (12 ounce) package shredded
   coconut

Combine first four ingredients in mixing bowl. Blend well, then stir in chopped pecans. Chill for 5–10 minutes. Form mixture into 1-inch balls, then roll balls in coconut. Chill until ready to serve.

Peanut Clusters

½ cup semi-sweet chocolate chips   6 ounces dry roasted peanuts
½ cup butterscotch chips

In a glass bowl, microwave chocolate and butterscotch chips for 1 minute. Stir. Microwave 30 seconds longer or until chips are melted. Stir in peanuts. Drop by spoonfuls onto waxed paper. Let cool.

Quick 'n' Easy Fudge

1 (12 ounce) package milk chocolate
  chips
1 (14 ounce) can sweetened
  condensed milk

1½ teaspoons vanilla
1 cup chopped pecans or walnuts

In a saucepan, melt together chocolate chips and sweetened condensed milk.
Remove from heat. Stir in vanilla and nuts. Spread into 8x8 inch baking pan
lined with waxed paper. Chill until firm. Remove from pan and cut into 1-inch
squares.

Rocky Road Candy

1 pound milk chocolate
½ pound semi-sweet chocolate
¼ cup butter or margarine
1 teaspoon vanilla

½ pound mini marshmallows
1 pound walnuts or pecans,
    coarsely chopped

Melt chocolate and butter slowly in double boiler. Remove from heat; stir in vanilla. Add marshmallows and nuts. Pour into buttered pan. Chill until firm.

Toffee

1 cup pecans, coarsely chopped
1½ cups brown sugar
1 cup butter (no substitutions)

1 teaspoon vanilla
3 (7 ounce) chocolate bars

Spread pecans on buttered baking sheet. Set aside. In saucepan, cook brown sugar and butter until candy thermometer reads 290 degrees. Remove from heat and stir in vanilla. Pour over chopped pecans. Lay chocolate bars on top. Let chocolate soften, then spread chocolate evenly over toffee. Cool completely, then break into pieces.

Turtle Candies

1 cup pecan halves
36 caramels

½ cup milk chocolate chips,
   melted

Preheat oven to 325 degrees. Arrange pecans, flat side down, in clusters of four on greased cookie sheet. Place one caramel on each cluster of pecans. Heat in oven until caramels soften, about 4–8 minutes. Remove from oven. Flatten caramels slightly. Cool briefly, then remove from pan to waxed paper. Swirl melted chocolate on top.

Walnut Fudge

1 quart whipping cream
1 cup dark corn syrup

4 cups sugar
1½ pounds shelled English walnuts, warm

In heavy saucepan, mix whipping cream, corn syrup, and sugar. Boil until candy thermometer reads 235 degrees, stirring frequently. Remove from heat and whip vigorously until stiff, then stir in walnuts. Pour into buttered 9x13 inch pan. Let cool completely, then cut into 1-inch squares.

White Bark Treats

2 cups Cheerios
2 cups crisp rice cereal
1 cup dry roasted peanuts

1 cup colored miniature marshmallows
1½ pounds white almond bark or
    vanilla candy coating

In large mixing bowl, mix together first four ingredients. Set aside. Melt almond bark according to package directions. Pour over dry ingredients and stir well to coat. Spread mixture on waxed paper to harden. When set, break up candy into smaller pieces and store in airtight container.

Christmas is not a time or a season
but a state of mind.
To cherish peace and goodwill,
to be plenteous in mercy,
is to have the real spirit of Christmas.
If we think on these things,
there will be born in us a Savior and over us will
shine a star sending its gleam of hope to the world.

CALVIN COOLIDGE

Christmas Breakfast

Apple Oven Pancake

2 tablespoons butter or margarine
2 tablespoons brown sugar
¼ teaspoon cinnamon
1 medium apple, peeled and
    thinly sliced

2 eggs
½ cup flour
¼ teaspoon salt
½ cup milk
1 teaspoon vanilla

Heat oven to 400 degrees. Melt butter in pie plate in the oven. Remove from oven and brush butter up sides of pie plate. In small dish, mix together brown sugar and cinnamon. Sprinkle brown sugar mixture over butter. Layer apple slices over sugar. In medium bowl, beat eggs. Stir in remaining ingredients just until blended. Bake 30–35 minutes, then immediately invert onto serving plate. Serve with syrup, if desired.

Baked French Toast

¾ cup brown sugar
1 teaspoon cinnamon
½ cup butter
1 loaf French bread, sliced

6 eggs
1½ cups half-and-half
½ cup toasted pecans, chopped

In small bowl, mix together brown sugar and cinnamon. Set aside. Melt butter in 9x13 inch baking pan in the oven. Sprinkle one-third of sugar mixture into butter. Place bread slices in the pan. Sprinkle remaining sugar mix over bread. Beat eggs and half-and-half; pour over bread. Refrigerate overnight. In the morning, sprinkle pecans over bread. Bake at 350 degrees for 35–45 minutes. Serve warm with hot syrup.

Breakfast Pizza

1 pound pork sausage, cooked, crumbled, and drained
1 (8.5 ounce) can refrigerated crescent rolls
1 cup frozen shredded hash brown potatoes, thawed
¼ cup chopped onion

1 cup shredded sharp cheddar cheese
5 eggs, lightly beaten
¼ cup milk
½ teaspoon salt
½ teaspoon black pepper
¼ cup grated Parmesan cheese

Preheat oven to 375 degrees. Separate crescent rolls into triangles. Place triangles on ungreased 12 inch pizza pan with points toward the center. Press rolls together, sealing perforations. Create small rim around edge of crust. Sprinkle cooked sausage evenly over crust. Top with potatoes and onion. Sprinkle with cheddar cheese. Whisk together eggs, milk, salt, and pepper in small bowl. Pour egg mixture evenly over pizza. Sprinkle with Parmesan cheese. Bake for 15–20 minutes or until eggs are set.

Eggnog Waffles

2 cups biscuit mix
⅔ cup milk
⅔ cup eggnog

1 egg, beaten
2 tablespoons vegetable oil
Chopped pecans, optional

In medium mixing bowl, whisk together first five ingredients. In batches, bake waffles on hot waffle iron 5–7 minutes or until lightly golden. If desired, sprinkle with chopped pecans before baking. Serve with your favorite syrup or topping.

Festive Breakfast Casserole

½ pound bacon
½ cup chopped onion
¼ cup chopped green pepper
¼ cup chopped red pepper
12 eggs
1 cup milk

1 (16 ounce) package frozen hash
  browns, thawed
1 cup shredded Colby-Jack cheese
1 teaspoon salt
½ teaspoon pepper

Preheat oven to 350 degrees. In skillet, fry bacon until crisp. Remove bacon from pan; crumble and set aside. In the drippings, cook onion and green and red peppers until tender. Remove from heat. In large mixing bowl, beat eggs with milk. Stir in hash browns, cheese, salt, pepper, bacon, onion, and peppers. Pour into greased 9x13 inch baking dish. Bake for 35–45 minutes.

German Potato Pancakes

6 medium potatoes, peeled and
    shredded
1 small onion, peeled and grated
2 eggs, beaten
2 tablespoons all-purpose flour

¼ teaspoon baking powder
1 teaspoon salt
¼ teaspoon pepper
¼ cup vegetable oil

Shred potato and onion. Place in colander and squeeze out as much liquid as possible. Working quickly so potatoes do not discolor, beat together eggs, flour, baking powder, salt, and pepper in large mixing bowl. Stir in potatoes and onion. In large skillet, heat oil over medium heat. Drop heaping tablespoonfuls of the potato mixture into the skillet. Press to flatten. Cook about 3 minutes on each side until browned and cooked through. Drain on paper towels.

Christmas is the season for kindling the fire
of hospitality in the hall,
the genial flame of charity in the heart.

WASHINGTON IRVING

Meats and Main Dishes

Baked Cornish Game Hens

4 Cornish game hens
½ cup butter, softened
1 teaspoon sage

2 cloves garlic, pressed
2 tablespoons lemon juice

Preheat oven to 350 degrees. Remove neck and giblets from hens. Rinse and pat dry. Rub hens with butter. In small bowl, combine sage, garlic, and lemon juice. Place hens in roasting pan and bake for 1 hour, basting with lemon mixture every 10 minutes.

Cider Baked Ham

1 (6–8 pound) bone-in ham
Whole cloves

3 cups apple cider

Preheat oven to 325 degrees. Place ham on rack in roasting pan; score ham in diamond pattern with sharp knife. Stud ham with whole cloves. Pour apple cider over ham. Bake 20 minutes per pound of meat until meat thermometer inserted in ham reads 160 degrees, basting every half hour with cider. Let ham stand for at least 5 minutes before carving

Dr. Pepper Glazed Ham

1 (2 liter) bottle Dr. Pepper, divided
1 tablespoon ground cloves
1 teaspoon cinnamon

1 fully-cooked ham, 7–10 pounds
Whole cloves

Place ham in roasting pan and cover with mixture of Dr. Pepper and spices. Bake ham for 1½ hours in a 325 degree oven. Remove from oven and score top of ham. Stud ham with cloves.

Mix together:

1 teaspoon cinnamon   1 teaspoon dry mustard

Add enough Dr. Pepper to form a paste. Brush mixture over scored ham.

Mix together:

1 cup brown sugar   ¼ cup Dr. Pepper or enough to form a paste

Brush final mixture over ham. Bake an additional 1½ hours or until ham reaches an internal temperature of 140 degrees.

Cranberry Chicken

6 boneless skinless chicken breast
    halves
1 can whole-berry cranberry sauce
1 large Granny Smith apple,
    peeled and diced

½ cup raisins
1 teaspoon orange zest
¼ cup chopped walnuts
1 teaspoon curry powder
1 teaspoon ground cinnamon

Place chicken in greased 9x13 inch baking dish. Bake at 350 degrees for 20 minutes. While chicken is cooking, combine remaining ingredients. Spoon cranberry mixture over chicken. Return to oven for 20–25 minutes or until chicken juices run clear.

Garlic Prime Rib

1 (10 pound) prime rib roast   5 cloves garlic, minced
Salt and black pepper to taste   ½ cup Dijon mustard

Preheat oven to 500 degrees. Score roast. Season with salt and pepper. In small bowl, combine garlic and mustard. Spread garlic mixture over roast. Place roast in roasting pan and cover. Roast for 1 hour, then turn off oven. Leave oven door closed for 90 minutes, then test internal temperature of roast. For a medium-rare roast, the temperature should be at least 140 degrees; medium should be 155 degrees.

Italian Turkey

1½ pounds salt pork, ground
1 clove garlic, minced
3 teaspoons ground sage

2½–3⅓ teaspoons chili powder
Salt and pepper, to taste
1 (10–12) pound turkey

Combine first six ingredients and spread over turkey. Bake 4½ hours or until done. Remove pork mixture from turkey and place in large mixing bowl; crumble mixture with a fork. Debone turkey and chop meat into small pieces. Blend turkey with pork mixture. Serve as loose meat or on rolls as sandwiches.

Mustard Glazed Ham

1 fully cooked ham, 8–10 pounds
1 small jar apple jelly
1 small jar pineapple preserves

1 (1 ounce) container dry mustard
2 tablespoons prepared horseradish
Salt and pepper

Bake ham at 325 degrees for 1 hour 45 minutes. Combine remaining ingredients and brush over ham. Return ham to oven for 35–45 minutes or until ham reaches 140 degrees.

Roast Duck

1 (4–5 pound) whole duck
2 teaspoons salt
1 teaspoon black pepper

2 teaspoons paprika
½ cup butter, melted

Preheat oven to 375 degrees. Remove neck bone and giblets from duck. Wash duck and pat dry. Rub salt, pepper, and paprika into the skin. Place in a roasting pan. Roast for 1 hour. Brush half of the melted butter over duck, and continue cooking for an additional 45 minutes. Brush remaining butter over duck and cook for 15 minutes longer or until skin is golden brown.

Traditional Christmas Turkey

1 (10–12 pound) whole turkey
6 tablespoons butter, sliced into
    pieces
4 cups warm water
3 cubes chicken bouillon

2 tablespoons dried parsley
2 tablespoons dried minced onion
2 tablespoons seasoned salt
2 tablespoons poultry seasoning

Preheat oven to 350 degrees. Rinse and wash turkey. Remove neck and discard giblets. Place turkey in roasting pan. Separate the skin over the breast and place slices of butter between the skin and breast meat. In medium bowl, dissolve bouillon in water. Stir in parsley and minced onion and pour mixture over top of turkey. Sprinkle turkey with seasoned salt and poultry seasoning. Cover with foil and bake 3½–4 hours, until internal temperature of turkey reaches 180 degrees. Remove foil during last 45 minutes to brown turkey.

Blessed is the season which engages
the whole world in a conspiracy of love.

HAMILTON WRIGHT MABIE

Pies and Desserts

Chocolate Cheesecake Pie

1 (8 ounce) package cream cheese, softened
1 (14 ounce) can sweetened condensed milk
1 cup semi-sweet chocolate chips, melted
2 eggs
1½ teaspoons vanilla extract
1 (9 inch) prepared chocolate cookie crust

Preheat oven to 350 degrees. In mixing bowl, beat cream cheese until fluffy. Gradually add sweetened condensed milk and melted chocolate chips. Beat in eggs and vanilla. Pour into prepared crust and bake 30–35 minutes or until set. Cool completely, then chill before serving.

Chocolate Chip–mallow Pie

24 large marshmallows
½ cup milk
1 cup whipping cream, whipped
1 teaspoon vanilla

1 cup mini semi-sweet or milk
    chocolate chips
1 prepared chocolate cookie crust

Over low heat, heat marshmallows and milk until marshmallows are melted. Cool completely. Fold in whipping cream, vanilla, and chocolate chips. Pour into cookie crust and chill.

Chocolate Pecan Pie

1½ cups coarsely chopped pecans
1 cup semi-sweet chocolate chips
1 (8 inch) pie shell, partially baked
½ cup light corn syrup

½ cup sugar
2 eggs, lightly beaten
¼ cup butter, melted

Preheat oven to 325 degrees. Sprinkle pecans and chocolate chips into pie shell. In a mixing bowl, combine corn syrup, sugar, eggs, and butter. Mix well. Slowly pour mixture over pecans and chocolate. Bake for 1 hour.

Christmas Angel Pie

1 (14 ounce) can sweetened
   condensed milk
⅓ cup lemon juice
1 (10 ounce) package frozen raspberries,
   thawed and drained

½ pint whipping cream, whipped
1 prepared graham cracker or
   shortbread crust

Stir together sweetened condensed milk and lemon juice. Fold in raspberries and whipped cream. Pour into prepared crust and chill.

Pumpkin Pecan Pie

1 (15 ounce) can pumpkin
1 cup sugar
½ cup dark corn syrup
1 teaspoon vanilla
1 cup pecan halves

½ teaspoon cinnamon
¼ teaspoon salt
3 eggs
1 (9 inch) unbaked piecrust

Preheat oven to 350 degrees. In large mixing bowl, blend together first seven ingredients. Add eggs and mix well. Pour into unbaked piecrust and top with additional pecans. Bake for 40–50 minutes or until a knife inserted 1 inch from edge of pie comes out clean.

Quick Cherry Cheese Pie

1 (8 ounce) package cream cheese,
  softened
½ cup powdered sugar
1 can cherry pie filling

1 (8 ounce) carton whipped
  topping, thawed
1 prepared graham cracker crust

Beat cream cheese and powdered sugar until well combined. Fold in whipped topping. Pour into graham cracker crust and top with pie filling. Chill.

Raisin Cream Pie

1 cup raisins
1 cup sugar
2 tablespoons flour
Salt

1 cup evaporated milk
2 egg yolks, beaten
1 teaspoon vanilla
1 (9 inch) piecrust, baked

Place raisins in saucepan and cover with water. Simmer until water has evaporated and raisins have plumped. Set aside. In large mixing bowl, mix together sugar, flour, and a dash of salt. Add evaporated milk and egg yolks and whisk until mixture is well blended. Pour mixture into saucepan and cook over medium heat until thickened. Remove from heat and stir in vanilla and raisins; cool completely. Pour into prepared piecrust. Top with meringue and bake in preheated 350 degree oven for 20 minutes or until lightly browned.

MERINGUE:

2 egg whites, room temperature   1 teaspoon cream of tartar

6 tablespoons sugar

Beat egg whites until frothy. Mix sugar with cream of tartar; slowly add to eggs a tablespoon at a time while continuing to beat. Beat egg whites until stiff peaks form. Spoon over raisin filling.

Traditional Pumpkin Pie

1 (15 ounce) can pumpkin
1 (14 ounce) can sweetened
    condensed milk
2 eggs, lightly beaten
1 teaspoon ground cinnamon

½ teaspoon ground ginger
½ teaspoon ground nutmeg
¼ teaspoon ground cloves
½ teaspoon salt
1 (9 inch) unbaked piecrust

Preheat oven to 425 degrees. Whisk pumpkin, sweetened condensed milk, eggs, spices, and salt in medium bowl until smooth. Pour into unbaked crust. Bake 15 minutes, then reduce oven temperature to 350 degrees and continue baking 35–40 minutes or until knife inserted 1 inch from edge comes out clean. Cool.

White Christmas Pie

1 tablespoon unflavored gelatin
¼ cup cold water
⅓ cup sugar
3 tablespoons flour
1½ cups milk
1 teaspoon vanilla

3 egg whites
½ teaspoon cream of tartar
½ cup sugar
1 cup shredded coconut
1 (9 inch) piecrust, baked

In small bowl, dissolve gelatin in cold water. Set aside. In medium saucepan, whisk ⅓ cup sugar and flour into milk. Cook until thickened. Remove from heat and stir in vanilla and gelatin; cool. In a mixing bowl, beat egg whites, cream of tartar, and ½ cup sugar until stiff peaks form. Fold into gelatin mixture. Carefully fold in coconut and pour into prepared piecrust. Chill.

Bread Pudding

4 cups milk
3 cups cubed bread
3 eggs, beaten
½ cup sugar

¼ teaspoon salt
1 teaspoon vanilla
2 tablespoons butter, melted

Scald milk; pour over bread cubes and let stand for 10 minutes. Beat eggs, then beat in sugar, salt, and vanilla. Pour over milk and bread. Drizzle melted butter over top and stir to combine. Pour into buttered baking dish. Bake at 350 degrees for 1½ hours or until set. Serve with custard sauce.

CUSTARD SAUCE:
1 cup milk
2 tablespoons sugar
Salt

⅛ teaspoon cinnamon
2 egg yolks, beaten

Bring milk to a boil. In small bowl, beat sugar, dash of salt, and cinnamon into egg yolks. Whisk egg mixture into boiling milk. Remove from heat. Chill before serving over bread pudding.

Butterscotch Apple Cobbler

1 (11 ounce) package butterscotch
   chips
¼ cup brown sugar
¼ cup flour

½ teaspoon cinnamon
2½ pounds tart apples, peeled,
   and sliced

Preheat oven to 375 degrees. In small bowl, combine butterscotch chips, brown sugar, flour, and cinnamon. Set aside. Layer sliced apples in greased 9x13 inch baking dish and sprinkle with butterscotch mixture. Bake 20 minutes. Remove from oven and sprinkle with topping.

TOPPING:

½ cup flour
¼ cup brown sugar
¼ cup butter

1 cup pecans, coarsely chopped
¾ cup quick-cooking oats

Combine flour and brown sugar, then cut in butter until crumbly. Mix in pecans and oats. Sprinkle over apples and bake for 30–40 minutes.

Creamy Baked Cheesecake

¼ cup butter or margarine, melted
1 cup graham cracker crumbs
¼ cup sugar
2 (8 ounce) packages cream cheese,
    softened

1 (14 ounce) can sweetened
    condensed milk
3 eggs
¼ teaspoon salt
¼ cup lemon juice
Fruit topping, optional

Preheat oven to 300 degrees. In small bowl, combine butter, cracker crumbs, and sugar. Press into bottom of buttered 9 inch springform pan. In large mixing bowl, beat cream cheese until fluffy. Add sweetened condensed milk, eggs, and salt. Beat well. Stir in lemon juice. Pour batter over cracker crust. Bake for 50–55 minutes or until cheesecake springs back when lightly touched. Cool completely, then chill. Serve with fruit topping of your choice.

Jiffy Layer Dessert

1 chocolate Jiffy cake mix
4 cups milk, divided
1 (3.9 ounce) package instant vanilla
  pudding
1 (8 ounce) package cream cheese, softened

1 (3.9 ounce) package instant
  chocolate pudding
1 (8 ounce) carton whipped
  topping, thawed

Preheat oven to 350 degrees. Mix cake according to package directions and bake in 9x13 inch baking pan for approximately 10 minutes. Cool. Mix vanilla pudding with two cups milk. Beat cream cheese until smooth; fold into pudding. Pour over cooled cake. Mix chocolate pudding with two cups milk and pour over vanilla layer. Frost with whipped topping. Chill.

Pumpkin Pie Dessert

1 (29 ounce) can pumpkin
1 cup sugar
1 teaspoon cinnamon
½ teaspoon salt
½ teaspoon nutmeg
½ teaspoon ginger
4 eggs, beaten

1 (12 ounce) can evaporated milk
1 (18.25 ounce) package yellow
   cake mix
1 cup chopped pecans
¾ cup butter or margarine, melted
Whipped topping, optional

Preheat oven to 350 degrees. Grease a 9x13 inch baking pan. In medium bowl, combine pumpkin, sugar, cinnamon, salt, nutmeg, and ginger. Add eggs. Whisk together until mixture is smooth. Gradually stir in evaporated milk. Transfer to prepared pan. Sprinkle dry cake mix over pumpkin mixture. Sprinkle nuts over cake mix. Drizzle with melted butter. Bake about 50 minutes or until top is golden brown. Cool in pan 2 hours before cutting. Serve with whipped topping if desired.

Layered Banana Pudding

1 (3.9 ounce) package instant
   vanilla pudding mix
1½ cups milk
1 (14 ounce) can sweetened
   condensed milk

3 cups whipping cream, whipped,
   divided
1 box vanilla wafers
3 bananas, sliced and dipped in
   lemon juice

In large mixing bowl, whisk together pudding mix and milk until smooth and
slightly thickened. Add sweetened condensed milk and beat until well blended.
Fold in 2 cups whipped cream. Chill. In glass serving bowl, begin with layer of
wafers, then ⅓ of sliced bananas, and ⅓ of pudding mixture. Repeat two times,
ending with pudding. Garnish with remaining cup of whipped cream and
crushed vanilla wafer crumbs if desired.

Rice Pudding

1 teaspoon butter
1 quart milk
1 cup cooked white rice
½ cup white sugar
¼ teaspoon salt

1 teaspoon cinnamon
2 eggs, beaten
1 teaspoon vanilla extract
½ cup raisins

Preheat oven to 350 degrees. Butter a 2-quart baking dish. In a heavy saucepan over medium heat, scald milk and remove from heat. Stir in rice, sugar, salt, and cinnamon. Mix well; slowly add eggs and vanilla. Stir in raisins. Pour mixture into prepared baking dish. Bake for 40 minutes, stirring halfway through cooking time.

Until one feels the spirit of Christmas,
there is no Christmas. All else is outward display—
so much tinsel and decorations.
For it isn't the holly, it isn't the snow.
It isn't the tree nor the firelight's glow.
It's the warmth that comes to the hearts of men
when the Christmas spirit returns again.

UNKNOWN

Soups and Salads

Baked Potato Soup

4 large baking potatoes, baked
²⁄₃ cup butter
½ cup onion diced
²⁄₃ cup flour
6 cups milk
½ cup shredded cheddar cheese

1 (8 ounce) carton sour cream
Salt and pepper, to taste
Additional sour cream, chopped
    green onions, cooked and
    crumbled bacon for topping

In large saucepan, melt butter. Add onions and sauté until clear. Add flour a little at a time and whisk into a paste. Add milk 1 cup at a time, whisking constantly; allow to thicken in between each addition. Cut potatoes in bite-sized pieces. When soup is desired thickness, slowly stir in potato pieces. Add salt and pepper to taste. Just before serving, mix in cheese and sour cream. Ladle into bowls and garnish with toppings.

Broccoli Cheese Soup

½ cup chopped onion
¼ cup butter or margarine
¼ cup flour
3 cups water
4 teaspoons instant chicken bouillon

2 (10 ounce) packages frozen chopped broccoli, thawed and drained
3 cups shredded cheddar cheese
2 cups half-and-half

In large saucepan, cook onion in butter until tender; stir in flour and blend well. Gradually stir in water; add bouillon and broccoli. Cook and stir until thickened and broccoli is tender. Stir in cheese and half-and-half. Cook and stir until cheese is melted and soup is heated through. Do not boil.

Corn Chowder

½ pound bacon
½ cup chopped onion
½ cup chopped celery
2 tablespoons flour
4 cups milk

⅛ teaspoon pepper
2 cans cream-style corn
Chopped fresh parsley
Paprika

In saucepan, fry bacon until crisp. Remove bacon from pan, crumble, and set aside. Drain fat, reserving 3 tablespoons in saucepan. Cook onion and celery in bacon drippings until tender; remove from heat. Stir in flour. Cook over medium heat, stirring constantly, until mixture is bubbly; remove from heat. Stir in milk. Heat to boiling, stirring constantly. Boil and stir 1 minute. Reduce heat. Stir in pepper and corn. Cook until soup is heated through. Remove from heat and ladle into soup bowls. Garnish with cooked bacon and a sprinkling of parsley and paprika.

Cream of Pumpkin Soup

1 cup chopped onion
2 tablespoons butter, melted
2 (14.5 ounce) cans chicken broth
1 (15 ounce) can pumpkin
1 teaspoon salt

¼ teaspoon ground cinnamon
⅛ teaspoon ground ginger
⅛ teaspoon pepper
1 cup half-and-half

In medium saucepan, sauté onion in butter until tender. Slowly add 1 can chicken broth; stir well. Bring to a boil; cover, reduce heat, and simmer 15 minutes. Transfer broth mixture into blender or food processor. Process until smooth. Return processed mixture to saucepan. Stir in remaining can of broth, pumpkin, and spices. Bring to a boil; cover, reduce heat, and simmer 10 minutes, stirring occasionally. Stir in half-and-half and heat through. Do not boil. Garnish as desired.

Broccoli-Cauliflower Salad

1 head broccoli
1 head cauliflower
12 bacon slices, cooked and
    crumbled
1 small red onion, chopped

½ cup raisins
½ cup sunflower seed kernels
1 cup mayonnaise
½ cup sugar
2 tablespoons vinegar

Chop broccoli and cauliflower into bite-sized pieces and place in large mixing bowl. Add bacon, onion, raisins, and sunflower seeds. In another bowl, mix together mayonnaise, sugar, and vinegar. Pour mixture over salad and stir until well blended. Chill overnight.

Buttermilk Salad

1 cup buttermilk
1 cup sugar
1 can pineapple chunks, drained

1 (8 ounce) carton whipped
   topping, thawed

Mix buttermilk and sugar well. Add pineapple and fold in whipped topping.
Spread in rectangular baking dish and cover with plastic wrap. Place in freezer
until frozen. When ready to serve, thaw for 20 minutes before cutting into
squares.

Cherry Delight

1 can cherry pie filling
1 can crushed pineapple, drained
1 (14 ounce) can sweetened
condensed milk

1 (8 ounce) carton whipped topping,
thawed
1 cup pecans, coarsely chopped

Blend first three ingredients. Fold in whipped topping and pecans. Chill overnight until firm. This can also be frozen.

Cinnamon Applesauce Salad

½ cup red hot candies
2 cups boiling water

2 (3 ounce) packages cherry or
strawberry gelatin
2 cups unsweetened applesauce

Dissolve candies in boiling water. Stir in gelatin and dissolve. Stir in applesauce. Pour into baking pan or gelatin mold and chill until firm.

Cranberry Salad

1 cup fresh cranberries, ground
1 cup sugar
1 (3 ounce) package lemon gelatin
1 cup boiling water
1 cup pineapple juice

1 cup crushed pineapple
1 apple, chopped
1 celery rib, diced
½ cup nuts, chopped

Combine cranberries and sugar. Dissolve gelatin in boiling water. Cool. Stir gelatin into cranberry mixture. Mix in pineapple juice, crushed pineapple, apple, celery, and nuts. Chill until firm.

Holiday Sherbet Salad

1 (6 ounce) package strawberry
  gelatin
2 cups boiling water
1 pint raspberry sherbet

1 (20 ounce) can crushed pineapple,
  drained
1 cup miniature marshmallows
1 (8 ounce) carton whipped topping

Dissolve gelatin completely in boiling water. Stir in sherbet. Chill until partially set, then mix in pineapple and marshmallows. Fold in whipped topping. Chill until firm.

Mixed Vegetable Salad

1 cup sugar
¾ cup vinegar
½ cup vegetable oil
1 teaspoon salt
1 can French-style green beans,
    drained

1 can shoe peg corn, drained
1 can small green peas, drained
3 carrots, grated
½ cup chopped onion
1 rib celery, sliced

In a saucepan, combine sugar, vinegar, oil, and salt. Bring to a boil. Remove from heat and cool completely. Combine remaining ingredients. Pour boiled mixture over the top and stir well. Refrigerate overnight.

Pear Salad

1 large can pear halves
1 (3 ounce) package lime gelatin
1 (8 ounce) package cream cheese

1 (8 ounce) carton whipped
   topping, thawed

Drain pears, reserving the juice. Add enough water to equal 1 cup. Heat juice and water and dissolve gelatin in it. Let it cool. Place pears and cream cheese in blender and process until smooth. Slowly add in gelatin mixture and blend well. Pour mixture into bowl and fold in whipped topping. Chill.

Pistachio Salad

2 (8 ounce) cartons whipped topping, thawed
1 (3.9 ounce) package instant pistachio pudding mix
2 cups miniature marshmallows
1 (20 ounce) can crushed pineapple, undrained
Additional chopped pistachios or pecans for garnish if desired

In large mixing bowl, blend whipped topping and pudding mix. Fold in marshmallows and pineapple. Sprinkle with nuts and chill.

Ritzy Orange Salad

60 Ritz crackers, crushed
½ cup butter, melted
½ cup sugar
2 small cans mandarin oranges
1 (14 ounce) can sweetened
   condensed milk

1 (8 ounce) carton whipped
   topping, thawed
1 (6 ounce) can concentrated
   orange juice, partially thawed

Mix cracker crumbs, butter, and sugar. Reserve ½ cup crumbs; press the remaining crumb mixture into an oblong dish. Reserving several orange slices for garnish (if desired), blend together the remaining ingredients until well combined. Pour over crumb crust. Garnish with reserved crumbs and oranges. Chill.

Joy to the world, the Lord is come!

Let earth receive her King;

Let every heart prepare Him room,

And Heaven and nature sing,

And Heaven and nature sing,

And Heaven, and Heaven, and nature sing.

Isaac Watts

Snacks and Appetizers

Bacon Quiche Bites

1 (3 ounce) package cream cheese,
   softened
½ cup butter, softened
1 cup flour
3–4 slices bacon, cooked and crumbled

2 tablespoons onion
½ cup shredded cheddar cheese
2 eggs
¼ teaspoon salt
½ cup milk

With a fork, blend together cream cheese and butter. Stir in flour. With fingers, work dough together. Form dough into a disk and chill. When firm, remove from refrigerator and divide into 24 balls. Press balls into the bottoms and sides of 24 mini muffin cups. Divide bacon, onion, and cheese between quiche shells. In small bowl, whisk together eggs, salt, and milk. Divide egg mixture between quiche shells. Bake at 350 degrees for 25 minutes. Cool for 10–15 minutes before removing from muffin pan.

Baked Water Chestnuts

1 can whole water chestnuts
½ cup soy sauce
Sugar

4 strips of bacon, cut in half
length-wise and width-wise

Drain water chestnuts. Marinate in soy sauce for 30 minutes. Drain sauce from water chestnuts and roll each water chestnut in sugar. Wrap each chestnut in strip of bacon. Bake in a 400 degrees oven for 30 minutes.

Blue Cheese Ball

1 jar Old English cheese spread
1 jar Blue Roka cheese spread
1 (8 ounce) package cream cheese,
    softened

1 small onion, minced
Worcestershire sauce
Chopped pecans

With a fork, thoroughly blend cheese spreads, cream cheese, onion, and a dash of Worcestershire sauce. Sprinkle chopped pecans onto a sheet of waxed paper. Spoon cheese mixture onto pecans. Roll cheese mixture in pecans and form into a ball. Wrap ball in plastic wrap and chill before serving with crackers.

Brie and Raspberry Pizza

1 (8 ounce) can refrigerated
   crescent rolls
8 ounces cubed Brie cheese

¾ cup seedless raspberry preserves
½ cup chopped pecans

Preheat oven to 425 degrees. Lightly grease 12 inch pizza pan. Unroll the crescent rolls and separate into triangles. Arrange in pan with points toward the center and lightly press seams together. Bake 5 minutes or until lightly brown. Remove from the oven and sprinkle with cubes of Brie. Spoon the preserves over the cheese. Sprinkle with pecans. Bake an additional 8 minutes or until the cheese is melted and the crust is golden brown. Cool 5 minutes and cut into wedges.

Christmas Cheese Ball

1 (8 ounce) package cream cheese
2 cups shredded cheddar cheese
2 green onions, chopped

1 (2 ounce) jar diced pimientos,
   drained
2 teaspoons Worcestershire sauce
1 teaspoon lemon juice

In a mixing bowl, beat together ingredients until smooth. Spoon mixture into small bowl lined with plastic wrap. Chill until firm. When ready to serve, invert onto a plate. Serve with crackers.

Hot Artichoke and Spinach Dip

½ cup sour cream
½ cup mayonnaise
½ cup grated Parmesan cheese
½ cup mozzarella cheese

1–2 teaspoons minced garlic
1 package frozen spinach, thawed
   and well drained
1 (14 ounce) can artichoke hearts

Preheat oven to 325 degrees. Combine all ingredients. Place in shallow casserole dish. Bake for 15–20 minutes or until bubbly.

Hot Ham 'n' Swiss Dip

1 (8 ounce) package cream cheese,
   softened
⅔ cup mayonnaise
1 tablespoon spicy brown mustard
1½ cup diced fully cooked ham

1 cup grated Swiss cheese
¾ cup cracker crumbs
2 tablespoons melted butter or
   margarine

Preheat oven to 400 degrees. Beat cream cheese and mayonnaise until smooth. Add mustard and blend well. Stir in ham and cheese. Spread into pie plate. In small bowl, mix together cracker crumbs and butter. Sprinkle cracker crumbs over dip mixture. Bake for 12–15 minutes.

Hot Ryes

1 cup finely grated Swiss cheese
¼ cup cooked crumbled bacon
1 (4½ ounce) can black olives,
    chopped

¼ cup minced onion
1 teaspoon Worcestershire sauce
¼ cup mayonnaise
1 loaf party rye bread

Preheat oven to 375 degrees. Mix first six ingredients together. Spread 2–3 teaspoons of mixture on slices of bread. Bake for 10–15 minutes or until bubbly.

Meatballs in Cranberry Sauce

1 can jellied cranberry sauce
1 bottle chili sauce
2 tablespoons brown sugar

1 teaspoon lemon juice
1 package frozen prepared
    meatballs, thawed

Preheat oven to 375 degrees. Blend first four ingredients until well combined. Place meatballs in greased baking dish. Cover with sauce, being sure to cover all meatballs. Bake until sauce bubbles.

Olive Cheese Balls

4 tablespoons butter, softened
2 cups shredded sharp cheddar
　　cheese
1 cup flour

¼ teaspoon salt
Cayenne pepper to taste
1–2 teaspoons water
50 whole ripe black olives

Preheat oven to 400 degrees. Cream butter and cheese. Stir in flour, salt, and cayenne; blend well. Mix in water and blend until dough holds together. Wrap each olive in dough and place on ungreased cookie sheet. Bake for 15 minutes.

Pineapple Cheese Ball

2 (8 ounce) packages cream cheese, softened
½ cup minced celery
¼ cup finely chopped green bell pepper
2 tablespoons minced green onion

1 (8.5 ounce) can crushed pineapple, well drained
2 tablespoons seasoned salt
2 cups chopped pecans, divided

In medium mixing bowl, combine cream cheese, celery, pepper, onion, crushed pineapple, seasoned salt, and 1 cup pecans. Divide the mixture in half and form it into two balls. Roll each ball in pecans. Chill overnight to let flavors blend.

Ranch Oyster Crackers

½ cup vegetable oil
¼ teaspoon garlic powder
¼ teaspoon lemon pepper
½ teaspoon dill weed

1 (1 ounce) package ranch dressing
   mix
1 (12 ounce) package oyster
   crackers

Preheat oven to 275 degrees. Thoroughly blend together first five ingredients
with a whisk. Pour mixture over oyster crackers and stir to coat. Place crackers on
a baking sheet and spread evenly. Bake for 15–20 minutes, stirring once halfway
through. Cool completely before storing in airtight container.

Shrimp Spread

2 (8 ounce) packages cream cheese, softened
½ cup mayonnaise
½ cup lemon juice
1 tablespoon prepared horseradish

2 (4.5 ounce) cans cocktail shrimp, rinsed, drained, and chopped
1–2 tablespoons finely chopped green onion
⅛ teaspoon garlic salt

In mixing bowl, beat cream cheese until fluffy. Beat in mayonnaise and lemon juice. Stir in shrimp, then add remaining ingredients. Refrigerate to blend flavors, then serve with crackers or vegetables.

Stuffed Mushrooms

4 cartons fresh mushrooms
3 green onions, chopped
1 (8 ounce) package cream cheese

1 egg
$\frac{1}{8}$ teaspoon garlic powder
Parmesan cheese

Clean mushrooms and remove stems from caps. Set caps aside and chop stems thoroughly. Mix stems, onions, cream cheese, egg, and garlic powder. Fill each cap with approximately 2 teaspoons mushroom mixture. Sprinkle with Parmesan cheese and bake at 350 degrees until tops are browned.

Stuffed Tomato Bites

2 pints cherry tomatoes
1 (8 ounce) package cream cheese, softened

6 bacon slices, cooked and crumbled
2 green onions, minced
1 teaspoon dried parsley

Slice off a thin layer from the top of each tomato. Scoop out pulp and discard it. Drain tomatoes well. In small bowl, beat together cream cheese, crumbled bacon, onions, and parsley. Spoon or pipe into tomato shells. Chill.

I heard the bells on Christmas Day

Their old familiar carols play,

And wild and sweet the words repeat

Of peace on earth, good will to men.

HENRY WADSWORTH LONGFELLOW

Vegetables and Sides

Asparagus Rice Casserole

1/4 cup butter or margarine, melted
1/2 cup slivered almonds
1 cup cooked rice
1 can cream of mushroom soup

1/2 cup milk
1 (15 ounce) can asparagus
1 cup grated sharp cheddar cheese
1 cup crisp rice cereal

Preheat oven to 300 degrees. Pour melted butter into casserole dish. Add almonds to dish and place in oven until lightly toasted. Add rice to almonds and mix well. In small bowl, blend mushroom soup with milk. Pour over rice mixture. Lay asparagus spears over soup and gently press down. Top with cheese, then cereal. Bake for 30–40 minutes or until bubbly and heated through.

Baked Potato Casserole

4 large baking potatoes, baked
   and cubed
1 pound bacon, fried and crumbled
1 (8 ounce) carton sour cream

4 ounces cream cheese, softened
1 cup shredded cheddar cheese
4 green onions, chopped
Salt and pepper to taste

Preheat oven to 350 degrees. Blend ingredients well. Bake until heated through
and cheese is melted, approximately 30 minutes.

Corn Bread Stuffing

CORN BREAD:

1¼ cups flour
¾ cup cornmeal
¼ cup sugar
2 teaspoons baking powder

½ teaspoon salt
1 cup milk
¼ cup vegetable oil
2 eggs, beaten

Preheat oven to 400 degrees. In mixing bowl, blend together dry ingredients. Stir in milk, oil, and eggs. Pour into greased 8 or 9 inch square baking dish and bake for 20–25 minutes. Cool.

STUFFIING:

1 pound fresh mushrooms, sliced
1 cup chopped celery
¾ cup chopped onion
½ cup butter
1⅔ cups water

4 chicken-flavored bouillon cubes
1 pound sausage, browned and
    drained
1½ teaspoons poultry seasoning

Sauté mushrooms, celery, and onion in butter until tender. Add water and bouillon cubes; cook until bouillon is completely dissolved. Set aside to cool. In large mixing bowl, crumble corn bread. Pour in mushroom mixture and remaining ingredients. Mix well. Bake at 350 degrees for 30–40 minutes.

Cheesy Veggie Casserole

2 bags frozen
broccoli/cauliflower/carrot
mixture, thawed

1 pound processed cheese, cubed
1 roll Ritz crackers, crushed
½ cup butter, melted

Preheat oven to 350 degrees. Pour vegetables into greased baking dish. Add cheese and distribute evenly. Sprinkle crushed crackers over vegetables and cheese and drizzle with melted butter. Bake for 35–40 minutes or until cheese is melted and bubbly.

Corn Casserole

1 can whole kernel corn, drained
2 eggs, lightly beaten
1 box Jiffy corn muffin mix

½ cup butter, melted
1 (8 ounce) carton sour cream

Preheat oven to 350 degrees. Combine all ingredients. Place in greased 9x9 inch baking pan. Bake for 45–50 minutes or until golden brown.

Creamed Carrot Bake

2 pounds carrots, peeled and sliced
2 (3 ounce) packages cream cheese,
   softened

¼ cup butter
2 teaspoons sugar
1 package stuffing mix

Preheat oven to 350 degrees. Cook carrots in salted water until tender. Drain well. Combine cream cheese, butter, and sugar. Carefully stir carrots into cream cheese mixture. Pour into 1½-quart buttered casserole dish. Sprinkle with dry stuffing mix. Bake for 20 minutes or until heated through.

Creamy Corn

1 (20 ounce) package frozen corn
1 (8 ounce) package cream cheese
½ cup butter

3 teaspoons sugar
6 tablespoons water

Place corn, cream cheese, butter, sugar, and water in slow cooker. Cook on low for 4–5 hours.

Green Beans Almondine

4 slices bacon
½ cup sugar
½ cup vinegar
1 medium onion, sliced thin

2 (15 ounce) cans green beans,
  drained
½ cup slivered almonds

In skillet, fry bacon until crisp. Set aside. Add sugar and vinegar to bacon drippings. Separate the onion into rings and place in skillet, then add beans and almonds. Cover and simmer for 25 minutes. Place in serving dish and sprinkle with crumbled bacon.

Onion Casserole

7–8 medium onions
½ cup unsalted butter
½ cup rice, uncooked

1 cup shredded Swiss cheese
⅔ cup half-and-half

Preheat oven to 350 degrees. Slice onions and sauté in butter until transparent. Boil five cups water and add rice. Cook rice 5 minutes; drain well. Mix rice, onions, Swiss cheese, and half-and-half. Transfer to a 2-quart casserole and bake for 1 hour.

Party Potatoes

10–12 medium potatoes, cooked
    and mashed
1 (8 ounce) package cream cheese
1 cup sour cream

2 tablespoons chopped chives
1 cup shredded cheddar cheese
Salt and pepper to taste
2 tablespoons butter

Beat together first seven ingredients. Place in greased 9x13 inch baking dish. Cover and refrigerate until 1 hour before serving time. Preheat oven to 350 degrees. Dot potatoes with butter. Bake for 1 hour or until potatoes are thoroughly heated.

Simple Bread Stuffing

2 loaves white bread
½ cup water
1 teaspoon chicken bouillon
1 small onion, chopped

2 teaspoons poultry seasoning
1 teaspoon salt
½ teaspoon ground black pepper

Cube bread. Lay cubes out on cookie sheet to dry out. When bread has dried, place cubes in mixing bowl. In small bowl, dissolve bouillon in warm water. Pour water over bread. Add onion, seasoning, salt, and pepper. Mix with hands. This can be used to stuff a turkey or can be baked in a greased casserole dish at 350 degrees for 1 hour.

Slow-cooker Ranch Potatoes

1 bag (24 ounces) frozen hash
  browns, partially thawed
1 (8 ounce) package cream cheese,
  softened

1 envelope (1 ounce) dry ranch
  dressing mix
1 can cream of potato soup

In large mixing bowl, mix ingredients together well. Pour into slow cooker and cook on low 6–8 hours or until potatoes test done and casserole is heated throughout.